Beyond Perfection

BUILDING A STRONG AND FULFILLING RELATIONSHIP

BEYOND PERFECTION
Copyright (c) 2024 by Edith Edem Agbeli

ISBN: 978-9988-3-7579-9

All rights reserved. No part of this publication may be reproduced, distributed, or transmitted in any form or by any means, including photocopying, recording or other electronic or mechanical methods, without the prior written permission of the publisher, except in the case of brief quotations embodied in critical reviews and certain other non-commercial uses permitted by copyright law.

For permission requests, write to the publisher via email to mzjudyed@gmail.com with the subject: **"Attention: Permissions Coordinator"**.

Ordering Information:
Special discounts are available on quantity purchases by corporations, churches, schools, associations and others. For details, contact the publisher with the details above or call +233 24 499 8789.

Designed and Printed by: Manifest Multimedia

Cover Art by: Obed Tawiah

CONTENTS

ACKNOWLEDGEMENT	i
THE BEGINNING	iii
MAKE YOUR SPOUSE A PRIORITY	1
ACCEPT YOUR DIFFERENCES	11
LISTEN CAREFULLY	
COMPLIMENT DAILY	19
WORK TOGETHER AS A TEAM	23
MIND YOUR MANNERS	29
WATCH LESS TV/SPEND LESS TIME ON SOCIAL MEDIA	34
HAVE TIME FOR FUN	39
DO THE LITTLE THINGS	44
CELEBRATE THE TOP FIVE	48
THINK POSITIVE	51
FIGHT FAIR	55
FORGIVE	59
WELCOME EACH OTHER HOME	65
GO TO BED AT THE SAME TIME/TOGETHER	69
DEVELOP MUTUAL FRIENDS	73
DATE TIME	79
MAKE LOVE	84
PRAY FOR YOUR SPOUSE	91
TREASURE YOUR SPOUSE	98
WRAPPING UP	102

ACKNOWLEDGMENT

This world is a better place, thanks to people who want to develop and lead others. What makes it even better are people who share the gift of their time to mentor future leaders.

To everyone I have had the opportunity to talk to, be led by, and lead, I want to say a big thank you for being the inspiration and foundation for this book.

Without the experience, support, and guidance from my family, friends, and the church, this wouldn't have been possible.

My main collaborator that has graced my life, Dr. Steve Stephens, a marriage psychologist, thank you.

To my husband, Charles Tsigbe, I have very little to say in words, thank you for the lessons.

My family, especially my parents, Dr. Theodore Kofi Agbeli and Gifty Acolatse, thanks for being my teacher and guide, staying together and showing me what love is all about.

To my Mum, Gifty Acolatse, for always being the person I could turn to during those dark and desperate years. You sustained me in ways that I never knew I needed. To my Dad, I am super grateful for the practical lessons.

To my elder sister, Cecilia Denanyoh, and brother, Edmond Agbeli; thank you for the support. I couldn't have made it this far without it.

My Friends who provided love, friendship, motivation, intellectual camaraderie, support, and conceptual organization, God bless you all.

Finally, to all those who have been a part of my getting there, that is true friendship, thank you.

Writing a book is harder than I thought, yet more rewarding than I could have ever imagined.

To every hurt, there was a lesson to be learned. In every conversation, there was knowledge to be derived from.

I conclude that many insightful writers in the marital field are correct. I hope my contribution will honor them all, adding a bit of precision and integration to the struggle to understand what makes close relationships work.

THE BEGINNING

Marriage, like everything on this earth, is governed by rules. While some may find these rules frustrating, most are in place to protect and help our society run smoothly. Surprisingly, the rules of marriage are simple, obvious, and incredibly powerful. By following these rules, your marriage can not only improve but also flourish and potentially save a struggling marriage.

It is important to not only learn these rules but also memorize and act on them. A successful marriage only requires two people who are both willing to make it work and give it an honest try. What makes a marriage work is surprisingly simple. Happily married couples are not necessarily smarter, richer, or more psychologically astute than others. Rather, they have hit upon a dynamic that keeps their negative thoughts and feelings about each other from overwhelming their positive ones. This dynamic is known as emotional intelligence.

Emotional intelligence is now widely recognized as an important predictor of success in various areas of life, including relationships. The more emotionally intelligent a couple is, the better able they are to understand, honor, and respect each other and their marriage. This, in turn, increases the likelihood of living happily ever after.

Unfortunately, one of the saddest reasons a marriage dies is that neither spouse recognizes its value until it is too late. Too often, a good marriage is taken for granted instead of being nurtured and respected. Getting divorced or remaining in an unhappy marriage is not a trendy or harmless choice; it can have harmful effects on everyone involved, especially the children.

This book is filled with practical rules that have been discovered through research and personal life experience. Each chapter will explain one of these rules, with references to the Holy Bible for additional guidance. Space will also be provided for your comments and practice, showing you how to apply these rules in everyday life.

Most of the examples in this book are geared toward men. While women may make the home, it is ultimately the man's responsibility to cherish his wife and family, make time for them, and put in effort to maintain a beautiful home. If one person in the marriage feels they are constantly putting in more effort than the other, trouble may be looming.

In summary, marriage rules may not always be easy, but they are important for protecting and maintaining a healthy society. By following these simple yet powerful rules, you can improve your marriage and potentially save a struggling one. Emotional intelligence is key, and it is essential to nurture and respect your marriage before it's too late.

This book is filled with practical rules that have been discovered over the years through research and personal life experience. This is not to say I know it all. I am still learning, each day comes with its challenges, lessons, and its own experience and hopefully, I will also get better as time goes on.

Rules from professional and personal experience are important but the most important is how the holy bible interprets and advises one on that situation. Do not stray from its teachings.

Each chapter in this book will explain one of the rules and show you why it is important. References to the Holy bible will be made. Space will also be left for your comments and practice, that is, how to insert the rules into the ups and downs of everyday life.

Let's jump into the rules and watch our marriages grow stronger, deeper, better, more positive, and more beautiful.

Let me please state here that most of the examples are geared toward men.

For me, contrary to the statement that women make the home, I think it is rather the men. Women are vulnerable and will fall for a man once he treats her well. For a man to love and treat you right, it means he does care. You can't keep a man who doesn't want to be kept. Neither can you impress a man who does not want you? So, pardon my examples.

A man who wants a beautiful home will make efforts, cherish the wife and the family, make time and spend time. The moment one person is the marriage feels he or she is constantly putting in more efforts than the other, trouble looms.

MAKE YOUR SPOUSE A PRIORITY

Most women do not feel important to their husbands even though they might claim to love them.

If only my husband paid more attention to my needs, Doris lamented. He claims to love me but his work, friends and a tall list of other things always come first. I feel like he really does not care.

Yes, this is a normal complaint we all hear so often. Most men take better care of their cars, houses, etc. than their marriage. We expect our marriages to be on auto-pilot and work even without any effort being pushed into it. We take our spouse's feelings and actions for granted. The reality however is that if we don't take great care of our marriages and relationships, they will eventually stop working and collapse.

One of the saddest reasons a marriage dies is that neither spouse recognizes its value until it is too late. Only after the papers have been signed, the furniture divided, and separate apartments rented do the exes realize how much they gave up when they gave up on each other. Too often a good marriage is taken for granted as stated earlier rather than given the nurturing and respect it deserves and desperately needs.

To thrive, your marriage MUST be your number one priority …… on the top of your list. Not only that but your spouse should see and feel this every day. If your partner doesn't feel she is special to you, sooner or later she'll be tempted to find someone who does make her feel special. This might divide her emotional connection between you two. Women love attention so make her feel wanted and needed by you.

It is not easy to keep your marriage on top of your list when there are so many other things that demand your time: job, children, responsibilities……. whiles each of these has its place in your life, developing a healthy marriage life is most important and should be given more attention than other responsibilities.

Not surprisingly, happily married couples have a far lower rate of such maladies. Sometimes all that is needed for a healthier life aside regular checkups and eating nutritiously is peace of mind because both partners will look out for each other on the above.

People who stay happily married, live four more years longer than people who don't.

I realized at one point in my marriage I was too busy with work and school. I went to work the whole week and instead of being home for the kids and my husband over the weekend I went to school.

Upon second thoughts I knew I had to prioritize so I chose to spend quality time with the family. Not everyone can do this, but the most important thing is finding a balance between work and the family and making sure the family knows they matter most in your life.

I must state that a healthy marriage benefits other as well. *It is the best gift you can give to your children.* Knowing their parents are happy together creates a real feeling of security and stability for them. It lays the foundation for their love life in future.

Balancing the parent role and marriage role can be difficult, but the worst decision or mistake a parent can make is to allow their children to take priority over their spouse. This is what happens when the man starts not to pay attention to the woman, and she finds solace with the children. However, focusing primarily on the children can threaten your marriage stability and when the marriage loses its stability the children will suffer for it.

It is normal for parents to love their children, but when a spouse places the child at the top of the priority list, the other partner often begins to feel resentful towards the children and the spouse. Whiles most women are happy when they hear the news that they are pregnant, most men are not because of the feeling that they will be sharing the love of their wife with the children. Do not allow this to happen in your marriage. Make your marriage strong by letting your spouse know he is your number one priority, make her know her needs come first even before the children.

TOOL 1: Make a mental list of all the ways you can let your spouse know he is your number one priority. Be creative and implement them.

Prayer:

Dear God,

Please help me to set my priorities straight according to your word. Help me to love the one you have given me with all my heart even when I don't feel like it. When I get distracted by all that must be done, remind me to take the time and effort to communicate that my partner is my priority. Remind me always to follow thy wiill and not my own. Help me to only see my partner instead of being wooed by earthly pleasures in times when he pays no attention to me.

Forgive me for all the time I have ignored my spouse.

Forgive me for all the times I gave my spouse only what was left after everybody and everything else had had their share.

Teach me to be generous and less greedy, more sensitive and less selfish, more focused and less hectic.

Teach me how to show love to my spouse every single day.

Teach me to show them the kind of love my spouse understands

Amen

Practice
1. Let your spouse know she is on top of the list and nothing can change that or remove her from her rightful position.
2. Pray with or for your spouse every day so nothing can change his feelings for you.
3. Set the alarm 15 minutes early so you can cuddle up together and talk about the day ahead and if possible pray together.

ACCEPT YOUR DIFFERENCES

Kwame loves spending time with his friends. Every single evening after work he will meet up with his friends for a drink up and always come home late. Whiles his spouse will go home and wait for him so they can talk about their day and play with the children.

When they first married Kwame was not doing this so often but with time his true self came out and it was up to his spouse to accept these changes and adjust accordingly or tensions will build up and tempers will flare.

Kwame and his spouse here have to learn to set priorities right and find a balance that works.

Every couple has their issues and differences. Some spenders are married to savers, some well-structured persons are married to unstructured people.

Let's say God has a great sense of humor. He made us such that opposites attracts. Often, we get attracted to people who drive us crazy. These differences are normally the difficulties couples face in their marriages. Don't let the differences get the best of you. Don't begin to believe you are too incompatible to make your marriage work. The thing is we are all incompatible in some areas or another. If compatibility was the main criterion for a great marriage, everyone will give up. Sure, some couples are more compatible than others but that doesn't make their marriage better.

God knows that balance is important that is why he gave you a spouse that is different from you. Never try to pressure your partner into thinking of feeling or acting as you do. Instead, make an effort to understand and appreciate the differences. Nagging and grumbling make us bitter. Fighting breeds frustration. But if you relax and soak in the differences as a blessing, you will learn the act of flexibility and compromise. You will grow in maturity and the texture of your life will become richer. In the end, you will develop into a better person – a person of character and compassion.

Most conflicts are not about major morals or ethical issues but about different preferences. The Bible asks what causes fights and quarrels among you. It's simple, you want something but can't get it.

As we learn to accept that we won't always have to have it our way, marriage becomes a lot easier. After a while, we realize that most of our fights are either stupid or selfish. As you learn to respect each other's differences, you'll find that you aren't fighting as much and rather moving closer to each other.
As you begin to accept the different ways in which you and your spouse are different, you will begin to bond and love each other the ways you both wish to be loved. As you grow closer, the differences will no longer seem like such a big deal.

TOOL 2: Make a mental list of all your spouse's actions that are different from yours and see how you can complement them.

Prayer:

Dear Lord, thank you for making my partner just the way she is, with all her strengths, weaknesses, and, our differences. It is no accident that the two of us are together, yet there are days our togetherness is challenged by our differences.

Help me to accept what you have given me. Help me to rejoice in our differences rather than merely tolerating them.

Forgive me for the many times I have been less than respectful — those times I have not paid proper attention or have not acted upon my spouse's words and ways which were different from my own.

Help us to understand each other and help us to live happily and as an example.

Amen.

Practice

1. Thank your partner for all the differences.
2. Try and see issues from your spouse's perspective the next time an argument comes up and try doing things his way.
3. Smile at the challenges, talk about them, and move on, life is short and must be enjoyed together .

LISTEN CAREFULLY

This seems simple enough but at times all of us have trouble listening. Listening means stopping what we are doing, looking at the person involved and truly hearing each word.

Most women complain that their husbands don't listen to them or take them seriously. People normally joke that if you want your secret kept, talk to your husband because he won't hear a word. So men please, pause the football game, turn down the television volume and listen to your spouse.

The problem with listening is most men and women are wired differently. Men like to get straight to the point and if the point isn't made in the first few sentences, their minds tend to wander. Wives should thus help their husbands by summarizing the major points of the story in the first paragraph. Tell the who, where, when, and what in the first sentence. Then follow with the little details so that even if it is missed the major points have already been listened to.

You can also stop mid-way and ask a question like, 'what do you think" or "what should I do next?'. Wait patiently for a response and then listen without interruption until he is done talking. You can continue with your conversation and questioning but keep it simple and none exaggerated.

Men need to realize that their wives yearn to connect with them and to connect often means to talk and to communicate. If you don't listen or talk to your partner, they will start to assume you don't care about them or what they are saying. If this continues they might find someone to talk to and that causes a lot of problems in relationships.

If you don't listen, your partner might stop talking. He/she might grow silent and withdraw connecting from you completely. Once a partner withdraws, getting him/her to reconnect is the most beautiful part.

Communication should be an intimate activity. The more you talk to each other the more he/she will open their heart to you. As you spend time talking and listening to one another, the two of you will grow closer and begin to build a healthy, thriving relationship. It is through this that the two of you can become emotionally one.

Remember the dating days, when both of you will sit for hours, talking, listening, and basking in the glow of each other? You were quick to hear and slow to speak. You wanted so much to learn more about each other, so you will be clung to every word and were excited by all that you heard. You can return to that time. All it takes is to listen, to communicate often.

When listening, do not pay attention to just the words alone, listen to the tone of the voice, emotions, and mood. Listen to the fears, hopes, and hurts. Start by getting rid of your preconceived notions. Always listen as if you two just met.

There is so much more to learn every day. Always listen with young, fresh ears. You might be surprised by what you will hear.

Not listening is a relationship disease. It can kill your love and marriage. Many relationships have this disease but are not even aware of or making efforts to cure it. Not communicating can eat away at your marriage while you move through your life naively unaware that the danger is just around the corner. Their cure is however simple – *STOP – LOOK – LISTEN*.

Using this simple solution, you can block the disease of not listening, strengthen your relationship, and save your marriage.

Start today and listen carefully to your spouse. You will be amazed at how quickly this simple rule will bring a sparkle to their eyes.

> *Prayer:*
> *Dear God,*
> *Help me to listen – really listen.*
> *Help me to listen to you, God.*
> *Help me to listen to what is true, noble, and right.*
> *Help me to listen carefully and caringly to the special person/ partner you have given me. Forgive me for how often I have neglected the words, the heart, and the hurts of my beloved. Forgive me for being more focused on explaining or defending or disputing than on really listening. Remind me daily that showing I care is more important than proving I am right. Show me how to listen with my whole heart and full attention. Amen.*

Practice
1. Whenever your partner starts to talk to you, put down whatever you are doing and look them in the eyes. Make the efforts.
2. When your partner talks to you, practice repeating back to him/her what you have heard.

Passage
James 1:19
Be quick to listen, slow to speak, and slow to get angry.

COMPLIMENT DAILY

Everybody loves a compliment.

While we all enjoy receiving compliments, most of us aren't very good at giving them. Some people think of complimentary things but rarely share them for fear of sounding silly. Others aren't even sure how to give the compliment. Perhaps, they were never complimented as children and now they subconsciously carry on the pattern of silence. Still, others are simply too lazy. A good compliment takes work and some people don't have the time, energy, or inclination to make the effort.

If you are looking for ways to improve your marriage, you can start with a compliment.

There are many different compliments. While each type is appreciative, some will be more treasured than others.

i. Possessive Compliment: This is a superficial type of compliment but it provides a good place to start if you are not used to complimenting your spouse. Example - what an incredible car you have or I so much love your earring.

ii. Appearance Compliment: You look wonderful or the dress shows off your eyes. These are the more personal compliments and let the recipient know, you find him/her desirable. We all like to be complimented on our appearance, but it's common to receive this kind of affirmation more from friends and relatives than from our partners. The only sad thing is, we mostly want to hear this from our spouse............

If your spouse doesn't compliment your appearance, don't look for it elsewhere. Talk to your partner about how you wish to please them. Find out what you could do to encourage more of these compliments and then give them a try. On the other hand, if you have not complimented your spouse lately, it's time to start. Don't miss the perfect powerful opportunity to communicate your love and strengthen your marriage.

iii. Behavior Compliment: When your spouse does something good, kind, or sacrificial, what do you say? Too often a partner says nothing because they see it as normal and take each other for granted. The longer you two have been together or married the more you take each other for granted. Spouses do a lot that deserves appreciation. Most people want to be recognized for work well done, for example, managing the children or finances, getting the groceries, cooking, etc. not appreciating someone's efforts is discouraging.

iv. Character Compliment: some people are selfless and selfishly reach out to others to assist without wanting anything back. Compliments of character- such as kindness, courage, responsibility, or wisdom may be best but then again, any compliment is good.

Make a list of sincere and personal compliments for your spouse then every day offer at least one. It will make a difference, I assure you. You will encourage your spouse and you will make them smile. You will draw them closer to you and will in turn improve your marriage.

Prayer:

Dear God,
I have so much to be thankful for and yet so often I am better at complaining than showing my appreciation.
Give me a grateful heart.
Open my eyes to the many things my spouse brings to my life and make me a better person.
Open my mouth to share lovingly and humbly all the things I should speak much more often than I have.
Forgive me for all the opportunities I have had to compliment that I haven't even noticed.
Forgive me for the many compliments I have thought of but never spoken of.
Forgive me for the times I have spoken highly of my spouse to others but have not complimented him/her directly.
Amen.

Practice
1. Give your spouse one compliment on his appearance right now, then make it a point to look for things to compliment them every day.
2. Make a list of all the things your spouse has done this past week. Reflect on the energy and sacrifice these things took. Thank your partner for all the things he has been doing.
3. Share a compliment each day for at least 10 days.
4. When your partner is complimented in public, reaffirm the compliment- a compliment always sounds better from a partner or someone you love.

WORK TOGETHER AS A TEAM

Before I got married, I was of the perception that when two people love each other, marriage should be smooth and easy. I believed difficulties were a sign of crisis and that there should be no problem in a good marriage.

After being married for all these years I now believe, marriage is hard work - a couple has to stand together and struggle through a host of difficulties. I believe challenges are normal and that they are just simply something to overcome.

If you have the new car of your dreams, what do you do to keep it running smoothly? You have to change the oil, rotate the tires, keep your fluids topped off, and make sure you respond quickly when something doesn't sound right. Does that take work? Yes, it does. Everyone knows if you don't take care of the details, you'll pay the price. The same applies to marriage, if you want it to run properly, you have to take care of it. This means regular and consistent maintenance.

It is so easy for a couple to get out of sync and work against each other. Every couple needs to understand this concept and instead embrace the idea of becoming intimate allies. Allies communicate and defend each other. They coordinate their efforts and help each other out.

Marriage is like a three-legged race: try to push ahead without your partner's cooperation and you both fall. Work together and you both succeed.

Most of the time, in marriage, you sometimes forget you are on the same team as your spouse. Your spouse is not your enemy or your competitor. The two of you are one. If your partner wins, so do you. If your partner loses, you do too. Your fates are linked.

It's amazing what can be accomplished in your marriage when you work together. You cover one another's weaknesses and reinforce each other's strengths. When you stumble, the other helps you up. This is what marriage is all about.

In Genesis, we are told the two shall become one. This is what marriage is about. *Togetherness becomes 'twogetherness', when two me's submit to each other and become one 'we'.* As you do this, you become stronger, closer, more efficient, more in sync, less lonely, and less stressed. And as a bonus, your marriage will become much more enjoyable. As the two of you work together as a team, there are at least five important factors that need to be present.

a. **Commitment** – If two people are not solidly committed to each other, their marriage will soon fall apart. Trust is the foundation of a good marriage and trust begins with commitment. Each of you needs to know that your spouse is committed to you and your marriage. The traditional marriage vows are, "for better or for worse, for richer or for poorer, in sickness or in health, to love, to honor, and to cherish, until death do us part." This is true commitment. Be committed to honesty, faithfulness, and lifelong love.

b. **Communication** – Without communication, any team is in trouble. You must communicate your thoughts, ideas, plans, and opinions regularly. You also need to communicate your feelings, those joys and fears, and frustrations in your heart. *Communication is key to a good marriage. Communication forms the connection that allows you to understand each other and grow – Author H. Norman Wright.*

When communication grows quiet, your relationship will turn cold, distant, and unsatisfying.

c. **Coordination** – Without coordination, your marriage will face conflicts and tension; you will find yourselves working against each other. Coordination means figuring out a way to work together that uses both partners' talents and abilities. It doesn't mean competing with each other or letting one person do all the work. When your efforts are coordinated, life goes more smoothly and more is accomplished. Those who coordinate their efforts can complete plays, finish projects and create a camaraderie that knits hearts together.

d. **Consideration** – Without this, feelings are hurt and your dreams slip through your fingers. A lack of consideration is selfishness and selfish players undermine a team. The true team may show consideration for their partner's feelings, interests, needs, desires, and preferences. When you are considerate with your partner, communication, and coordination improve, and so does your marriage.

e. **Clarity** – Without clarity of vision, a team has no goal or direction. The players wander in circles or slip into the dreaded downward spiral. Dreams give us clarity. They energize us and motivate us and also give us hope. Someone once said, if you aim at nothing, you'll probably hit it. Don't let this happen to you. Dream big and dream together. Plan for the future with excitement and anticipation. Robert F. Kennedy once said, "Some men see things as they are and say, 'why not'"? A couple who is looking in the same direction can walk forward hand in hand with determination and satisfaction. We all need a dream, plus the passion and courage to peruse them.

As you and your spouse build and strengthen each other with these five factors, you will find you are working as a team. In doing so, you will also discover that:

Commitment + Communication + Coordination + Consideration + Clarity = Contentment

Marriage is hard work, but it is work done together. It is hard work done as the two if you remember that you are both one i.e. the same team, covering each other's back, helping each other's play, and sometimes even kneeling at each other's side.

Prayer:

Dear God,
Forgive me for the times when marriage was tough and I have not worked hard enough to make it better. Also, forgive me for all the times I have not worked together with my spouse to improve my situation.
Help me to see my partner as an ally and a teammate, even when we seem to be pulling in different directions.
Empower me to hold strong to a commitment that is total and timeless.
Teach me to practice good communication.
Show me all that can be accomplished through the coordination of our efforts.
Remind me of how consideration softens both of our hearts.
Encourage me to have a clarity of vision that fosters the wonder of dreams and helps those dreams become reality.
When all is said and done, teach me how to be the sort of teammate you want me to be.
Amen.

Passage

Colossians 3:23
Work hard and cheerfully at whatever you do as though you were working for the Lord rather than for people.

Passage

Colossians 3:23
Work hard and cheerfully at whatever you do as though you were working for the Lord rather than for people.

Practice
Colossians 3:23
Work hard and cheerfully at whatever you do as though you were working for the Lord rather than for people.

a. Go to the place that holds special memories for both of you and talk about the following commitments:
    - To never purposefully hurt each other
    - To protect each other
    - To be faithful emotionally and sexually
    - To keep promises
    - To be honest
    - To never mention divorce
    - To love and care for each other no matter what
b. Find something that the two of you can work on- this will make you spend time together.

MIND YOUR MANNERS

Most people are so polite and appreciative in their relationships whiles dating but once the wedding is over they become a different person. They forget to say "excuse me" "I am sorry" or "are you ok" or "thank you". Spouses become politer to strangers than their partners.

In Ephesians 4:29, "Do not let any unwholesome talk come out of your mouth. In Philippians 1:27, Apostle Paul makes a similar appeal, "whatever happens, conduct yourselves in a manner worthy of the gospel of Christ".

In recent years, our culture has become more casual in how we relate to one another, but in that casualness, we have forgotten our manners. We don't say 'please' and 'thank you'. We interrupt, we don't open doors for our spouses, and we don't let him or her go first. We get loud and pushy. We don't ask or listen. We have become oblivious to the needs of others. And the worse problem of all is that we even notice how offensive our lack of manners has become and we do nothing.

If you love your spouse, take a moment to consider your actions. Think about how you speak and act to him, and ask yourself the following questions:

a. Are you respectful or rude?

b. Are you polite or are you inappropriate?
c. Are you mannerly or are your crude?
d. Are you patient or are you demanding?
e. Are you curious or are you selfish?

By doing the above, you will be able to focus on the areas of your life that need some fine-tuning.
Three things in human life are important, 1 Corinthians 13:4: love is kind

a. To be kind
b. To be kind
c. To be kind

It is always important to mind your manners and be polite. If you are kind and polite to your spouse, she in turn will be kind, polite, and submissive. You plant the seed of disrespect if you don't mind your manners, you will reap what you sew, sooner or later, and those seeds will contaminate even the best-kept field of marriage.

One counselor has a unique approach to bringing couples closer together. He asks them to set their dinner tables with candlesticks and fine china. He tells them both to dress at their very best. The husband is to shave, splash on cologne and wear a suit and tie. The wife is to do her hair, put on makeup, and dress up. They are to light the candles and eat their meals. This according to him improves almost every marriage. Why? Because when we are dressed up, we tend to behave better.

People are politer when they look nice and are in a more formal setting.

When a husband and wife are rude, crude, insensitive, or inattentive towards each other, you know something is wrong. Yet when they treat each other well and show gentleness, patience, thoughtfulness, or caring towards one another, you know their marriage is probably very healthy. You say to yourself, there is a couple in love. You might even say, 'I wish we could be more like that'.

Sometimes in an attempt to improve our relationship, we create a list of all the things our spouse could and should do better. This strategy rarely works. The only thing it accomplishes is to make us more frustrated and discontented. I suggest you start with yourself. As you become politer and more kindhearted, sooner or later your spouse will notice. In time, it will start to rob off on him/her, probably not as fast as you wish it would, but if you are patient and consistent, things will improve. Unfortunately, most of us get tired and give up too soon. We nag and demand, threaten and decide to give him a little of his own medicine. In doing so, we become just as rude as he is, and things get worse instead of better.

Commit to starting with yourself. Start today to be politer and less demanding more considerate and less obnoxious, more generous and less hurtful, more attentive and less distracted, more thankful and less selfish. When you treat your spouse with positive regard, she soon begins to feel positive about herself, about you, and your marriage. Positive regards communicate acceptance, respect, and honor. Good manners do the same thing.

Another great way to mind your manners is to say 'I'm sorry'. For some reason, this seems especially hard for guys. The words are simple, but we don't say them nearly as often as we should. Good manners demand that you say, "I am sorry" whenever it is needed. So here are times to say, "I'm Sorry".

a. When you are wrong
b. When you are rude
c. When you are defensive
d. When you are impatient
e. When you are negative
f. When you are hurtful
g. When you are insensitive
h. When you are forgetful
i. When you are confused or confusing
j. When you have neglected something important to the one you love
k. When you have damaged something that was your partner's
l. When you have not said, "I am sorry" as sincerely or quickly as you should have.

These two words are not a cure-all for bad manners, but they certainly don't hurt.

Note: Where there is love, there are manners and where there are manners, there is the potential for a great marriage.

Prayer:

Dear God,
At times I can rude and insensitive. I get wrapped up in what I want and how I think life should be without any regard for my spouse's feelings.

Forgive me for the rudeness and the bad manners. Forgive me when I am so caught up in myself that I don't even notice my rudeness and bad manners. Forgive me when I try to justify or excuse my bad behavior.

Remind me of the right words at the right time so my words bring my spouse and me closer, rather than creating distance between us. Assist me in letting no unwholesome words come from my mouth. And when I blow it, give me the grace to apologize quickly and do what needs to be done to repair my foolishness.

Show me how to be kind and patient in the midst of this fast-paced, egocentric world I live in.

Teach me to mind my manners, dear God.

Amen

WATCH LESS TV/SPEND LESS TIME ON SOCIAL MEDIA

What are you watching? Belinda asked her husband, Emmanuel.

Nothing.

Then why don't you turn off it and join me in bed?

Emma: I probably should but there might be something better in a few minutes.

Belinda shook her head and walked away to spend another evening alone whiles her husband sat in his favorite chair, his eyes glued to the television.

Television isn't bad, but it can do bad things to your marriage. It can pull you apart and steal precious moments, filling them with irrelevant and sometimes highly questionable materials.
Social media just like television can hypnotize those who engage in it. Soon, you will find yourself absorbed by what you see and oblivious to what is happening around you.

Television obsessions come in a variety of flavors: sports fanatics, sitcom junkies, history buffs, soap-opera addicts, news nuts, reality shows, medical dramas, etc. Whatever your preference, you are probably watching more television than you need to watch. Therefore, here are a few rules that might help you to tame your television or social media habits.

1. Choose ahead of time what you want to watch, and only turn on the television when that show is started. Turn off the television when that program is over.

2. Decide how many hours of TV per day are appropriate for your family. Then discipline yourself to stay within those limits.

3. Same way decide how many hours a day to spend browsing your phone. Some applications can set limits for you.
4. Don't watch TV alone. Decide that you will only watch programs that you and your spouse both want to see. Sit together on the same couch and watch those shows together. If your spouse doesn't want to watch, don't watch also.

5. Talk about what you watch.

6. Find a show that you both enjoy, then once a week, set up a date and time to watch your special show. Make it a tradition that is fun and romantic.

Television viewing and social media browsing is time-consuming and must be controlled or they will control you. It draws you and won't let you go. It demands your attention and resents competition.

Music however is not so demanding. It equally has contents to shape your mood or merely set the atmosphere, allowing you to leave the room and return whenever you wish. Not only that but it intensifies intimacy, depends on connectedness and builds priceless memories.

Someone once said music is the soundtrack to our lives. Therefore, find music that touches you both, and then allow your home to overflow with sounds that nurture and refresh your soul. Fill your morning with uplifting and lively music. Listen to relaxing melodies in the evening. Keep a collection of your favorite romantic songs in your bedroom. When inspiring music is playing, you'll be less likely to turn on the television and allow your partner to spend less time with you.

As you learn to appreciate music together, look for songs or even one song that you both can call "our song". Imagine listening to "had I told you lately that I love you" by Van Morrison in the evening in a cozy environment………need I type more.

If you don't have one special song, you are missing out on something very special and wonderful. Think back to the songs that were meaningful during your courtship and marriage. Christen one of them as "your song" and then add others as they touch your heart. Never be so far away from the wonderful memories that add to the romance and intimacy of love.

Prayer:

Dear God,
Keep me from being so distracted by TV and social media that steals my time, time that would be much spent connecting with my spouse. Forgive me for the times I have not listened to or shown my love for my spouse because I was so consumed by a program or trending topic that means nothing in the light of eternity.

When I do watch TV, show me how to do it wisely and responsibly that doesn't build walls but rather builds a bond that can't be broken. Fill my marriage with beautiful music- positive, exciting, romantic music. And when the sad song comes, draw us into each other's arms. Send us special music that touches our hearts and strengthens our love. Give us a song that can truly be "our song"
Amen

Passage
Philippians 4:8
Fix your thoughts on what is true and honorable and right. Think about things that are pure and lovely and admirable. Think about things that are excellent and worthy of praise

Practice

1. Sit down with your spouse and read the five TV rules together. Determine to put each rule into practice for one week. After talking about the rules you will try to try for a full year.
2. Find some relaxing music that you both like and play it at the end of the day as both of you enjoy the closeness of each other's company.
3. Think back on all the meaningful songs you've heard in the course of your relationship. Or find songs that express your thoughts or feelings about each other. This you can present to your spouse as a gift.

HAVE TIME FOR FUN

When two people first meet, they are often drawn to one another by the fun they have when they are together. When my husband and I were getting to know each other, we laughed and play, and shared quality time talking. Everything from walking to spending quality time together, going to comedy plays, parks, and beaches, admiring each other and even going away on short vacations just to spend time together.

Before marriage, most couples know how to have fun. But once they get married, the stress of life builds. There are bills to pay and meetings to attend and responsibilities to meet. Before you know it, life becomes more serious. Then comes a house or children and unforeseen difficulties. Soon all the pressures of life begin to squeeze out much of the fun you once shared. There just isn't the time, energy, or money to have as much fun as you once had.

Far too often, married couples have often forgotten how to let loose and have fun.

When was the last time you and your spouse spent the day just having fun? Most will ask "how relevant is this in marriage"? Most couples are busy with work and kids and assume that is most important, but with time they realize they no longer have each other. We are sabotaging our marriages and don't even know it. When couples laugh and play together they are

are normally creating an emotional connection that is necessary to help them get through the conflicts and crises of marriage.

Sit down with your spouse, discuss having fun, plan it, budget it, and do it as having fun is a serious business in marriage.

Playfulness helps you to relax and when you can relax, you will find that you're able to relate to one another more positively. When the busyness and pressures of life get to you, your stress level builds. When you are stressed you become irritable, impatient, and negative. Having fun relieves stress and builds great memories.

Unfortunately, some people associate having fun and playfulness with immaturity. They seem to think that fun is something you outgrow. I hope I never outgrow playfulness, joy, and laughter.

One of the things that frequently blocks a couple from fun is that neither person is quite sure what to do. Here is an easy way to get started.

- Make a list of all the fun things that come to your mind. All the things that you keep telling yourself, "someday I'd do this/that, write it down.
- Think of things you have already done and already enjoyed.

Here are a few suggestions:
1. Plan out a dream vacation
2. Cook together
3. Dance in your living room
4. Play your favorite board game
5. Rent a funny video
6. Go to the movies

Life offers us thousands of adventures. Keep your list handy, and keep adding when you discover new things. Try and schedule one at least once every month with your spouse.

If by any chance you are still stuck and don't know what to do for fun, consider the simple pleasure of laughing. Every couple once in a while need a good loud laugh together. Listen up and develop a good sense of humor. A healthy couple uses humor to break up the tension, move closer together, build great memories, and have more fun. No matter how difficult a situation, builds great memories and more fun. No matter how difficult a situation is, laughter can help you get through it.

Laughter is good medicine. It heals the hurt and strengthens your marriage. When life is heavy, a sense of humor can make things seem better and lighter.

As the bible says in Proverbs 15:15, "a cheerful heart has a continual feast". A smile can make everything appear more positive. Laughter makes you feel better, it reduces stress and pushes away depression. It is also contagious.

If you want a great marriage, commit to having some fun. Be responsible and do what needs to be done, but wear a smile. Develop a cheerful heart and a sense of humor my mother always says. Play to your heart's content and laugh until your side hurts. Do what you did when you first met each other and your love was fresh.

Prayer:

Dear God,
Thank you for creating a world that includes time for fun and play and laughter. Teach us to have more fun. Forgive us for all the times we take life too seriously, letting the trials and troubles of each day blind us to the excitement and joy that surrounds us.

Help us to find a balance between hard work and solid play. Remind us that for the six days, you created and on the seventh day you rested. Show us how to rest, relax and play.

Place in our hearts a sparkling laughter that can lighten the heaviest burden. Give us a contagious enthusiasm for all that is good and right and pure. Let our laughter lift each other. Let it spread beyond ourselves to those with whom we come in contact, lifting their spirits and pointing them to the source of all hope.

Return us to the time in our marriage when fun and play and laughter seemed so natural.
Amen.

Passage

Ecclesiastes 3:1-4

There is a time for everything, a season for every activity under heaven. A time to cry and a time to laugh. A time to grieve and a time to dance.

Practice

1. Make a list of five to ten things you did before you were married that were fun. Reminisce with your spouse about these and schedule time together to do one thing on your list sometime in the next week.
2. If you are experiencing stress and difficulty in your life right now, talk with your spouse about the positive (or humorous) side of your situation. Pray together and thank God that he gives the good with the bad.
3. Rent a comedy video or go to a concert or find a book of humorous stories, then sit together and let yourself laugh and laugh and laugh.

DO THE LITTLE THINGS

One of the mistakes men keep making is thinking "the bigger the better". Meanwhile, most women simply want to know that their husbands care about them. When it comes to showing affection, a single rose can be as powerful as a dozen. A simple call to check on her or a common hug can go a long way.

Big plans can be nice, but more often, it's the little things that count the most. "Little movements towards our spouse that increases our contentment with each other"-John Gottman. It is the smile, the opening of the door, the backrub, the kiss on the forehead, the kind words or compliments, and her favorite ice cream that make all the difference.

Some people are givers, some are takers, and others are both givers and takers. Years ago, I was told the definition of a gift is giving someone what they want, whiles the definition of a present is giving something you want them to have. This means you have to take your time to find out what your partner wants and needs at each time.

- What things are important to your partner?
- What brings your partner joy?
- What are their hobbies and interest?
- What makes your partner smile?
- What will make their life easier?

Be proactive, and look for ways you can do the little things for your spouse every single day. *Be creative, be personal, and be generous.*

If your partner is the most important person in your life, then you can never give too many of anything, be it massages, a back rub after a stressful day, small love notes, flowers, etc. if you want to please your partner, that simply means paying attention to the details and then trying hard to remember them. You can keep a notebook purposely for this. The more you do for someone the more the person is also willing to do for you. As you do for each other, your love and appreciation will grow. Relationships and marriages are worth fighting for only if the other party is at the same fighting level.

One person cannot be putting in all the energy whiles the person consumes it.

I know of a couple who kept a susu box to collect all their coins at the end of the day. As the years passed they accumulated many jars of change and to their surprise, they had accumulated enough to take a vacation. Pesewas, small notes all add up, so do the good deeds. They soften the hard edges of life and compensate for our foolish mistakes. They build treasured memories and assure a positive relationship that will last "till death do us part".

Prayer:

Father, when I am tempted to get wrapped up in myself, help me to look beyond my wants and wishes, and needs. Forgive me for my selfishness. Give me the desire to make my loved one smile by giving generously to the little things of life that might require my time, energy, money, and planning.

Remind me that it is truly better to give than to receive.
Show me how to give freely and cheerfully and spontaneously. Make me more of a giver and less of a taker.
Teach me to give as You give.

Thank You for your abundant gifts and all the little ways you bring beauty, comfort, and wonder into my life.
Inspire me to do little things each day that will show my spouse that I deeply love them and appreciate all they do.
Amen.

Passage
Matthew 7:12
Do unto others what you would want others to do for you.

Practice

1. Find something special you can do for your spouse one day this week. Start simple. Does she love to be pampered? Does he like certain magazines or meals? Treat him or her to it
2. Take a few minutes to write done as many of your spouse's preferences or special interests as you can think of. If you are not in the habit of observing your spouse, you may be surprised at how few details you know. Keep the list accessible so you can update it as and when you learn more.
3. Watch other couples to see what little things they do for each other
4. Set aside special days so you can try as many of them as possible.

CELEBRATE THE TOP FIVE

Celebrations are ways of saying
1. I love you
2. You are special
3. I am glad I married you
4. You are appreciated
5. Thank you.

We all know we ought to be saying these words every day of the year, but it's easy to get distracted and wrapped up in the business of life. So, there are special days set aside on your calendar for these messages. Yet too often we don't take full advantage of these invaluable opportunities to strengthen our marriages.

I call these opportunities the "top five":

1. Christmas
2. Valentine's day
3. Wedding anniversary
4. Spouse holiday
5. Mother's/ Father's Day.

At any rate, these days give you chances to be a hero. If you put some time and effort into each of these, I guarantee your spouse will draw closer to you.

These days of celebration are chances to be generous and

giving. One of the easiest things you can give your spouse is a card.

On each of the top five holidays, you must give your partner a gift to show appreciation. There are no excuses, justifications, or explanations acceptable. I realize some years are tough and you might think is better not to exchange gifts. This is a big mistake. You should never miss an opportunity to boost your marriage. Besides there are lots of gifts you can give that cost little or no money.

Everyone loves gifts, even though some are better at receiving than giving. Yes, some years are tough and you might think is better not to exchange gifts on a particular occasion. That is a big mistake! You should never miss an opportunity to boost your marriage. Be creative and you might be amazed at what other inexpensive gifts you can come up with. It is often the homemade gifts that mean the most because your spouse knows you put time and effort into them.

Do something extra to make these special days more memorable and unique. Celebrate these days in a big way. But don't allow yourself to be limited by only the five above. Ake each day special, make each day feel like the last time together. Surprise your spouse by sending a simple appreciation card or create something memorable for no reason other than to say, you are special and I am thankful you are mine.

Prayer:

Dear God,
Teach me to be creative in showing my spouse how important he is to me. Help me to give generously as you have given to me. Help me to model the meaning of love in an extraordinary way. Help me to show appreciation for all the positive things my beloved has done and said. Help me to honor him specifically and selflessly for being who he/she is. Help me to applaud the way she/he has specifically loved, nurtured, protected, and trained the children.

In the midst of my hectic schedule, remind me to create a wonderful memory for the special partner you have graciously given to me. Amen.

Passage
Romans 12:10
Love each other with genuine affection and take delight in honoring each other.

THINK POSITIVE

Negativity is devastating. It sucks the life out of a marriage and can even leave to separation or divorce. Under normal circumstances, wives tend to point out their husbands' insensitivity, stubbornness, and silence but husbands usually stick to negativity when complaining about their wives. Men will normally say the following:

- "Nothing I do will make her happy"
- "No matter what I do, it's not good enough"
- "If everything I do is wrong, why try"

You must understand that most guys truly want to please their wives, but if they are regularly confronted with negativity, sooner or later they will give up. They stop disciplining the children, initiating sex, or talking to their wives altogether because they have simply faced too many negative responses.

Negativity is a tough habit to break too. There are so many ways you can be negative towards your spouse. You can be critical, enhancive, sarcastic, short-tempered, unresponsive, impatience, unhappy, sharp, nagging, defensive, the list goes on. Some are very skilled at being negative. Stress is a major factor that can steal your ability to be positive. This stress can come from work, finances, family, friends, or even a love life. But whatever its source, stress has a way of making life miserable. Among other symptoms of stress, three of the most common are:

- Impatience
- Irritability
- Intolerance of things you would normally ignore

If you find some productive ways to manage your stress, you'll probably begin to see a decrease in your negativity. When you start to feel overwhelmed, try a few of the following:

- Take a break
- Go for a walk or a drive
- Call a friend
- Read a book or magazine
- Write a journal
- Exercise
- Count your blessing
- Find something that relaxes you
- Mental filtering.

Thinking positively isn't just about avoiding stress, it requires you to focus on the best qualities of life. The key is to focus on whatever is true, noble, pure, lovely, admirable, and praiseworthy. In any marriage, there are going to be disappointments, hurts, and frustrations. If you focus on these, I guarantee you will be more negative.

We all know we are attracted to positive people and tend to avoid those that are negative. Let's make an effort to smile, joke and encourage our spouse. It will make you more attractive and you might be surprised at how it can make a difficult situation beautiful.

"You can either complain that rose bushes are thorns or rejoice that thorn bushes are roses" - *Philosopher Ziggy*

Prayer:

Dear God,
Life is sometimes hard, but you are always good. Circumstances are sometimes overwhelming but you are always in control. Marriage is sometimes difficult but you always provide strength, wisdom, and hope. Teach me to be content with whatever situation I find myself in.
Help me not to make the stress of each day make me negative.
Show me ways not to correct my negative thinking so it does not steal my joy. Forgive me for all the times I have let a negative attitude get the best of me and made me hurt or discourage those whom I love the most.
Thank you for giving me these positives to list my spirit.
Amen

Passage
1 Thessalonians 5:18
No matter what happens, always be thankful for this is God's will for you who belong to Jesus Christ.

> **Passage**
> Talk to your spouse about the times in your marriage when you have been mostly negative, the trigger, and work on how to avoid it in the future.
>
> Make a goal to stay positive as much as possible and for your spouse to remind you when you fall short.

FIGHT FAIR

Every couple fights. Some couples fight frequently, while others only disagree once in a while. Some battle with silence, while others are loud. Some explode and then it's over, others pick and complain for years. Research shows that a person's fighting skills resemble that of animals.

A turtle: you withdraw inside yourself.

A deer: you get away as fast as you can.

A shark: you go for blood.

A donkey: you stand your ground and don't budge.

A chameleon: you give them whatever you want.

An elephant: you give in, but you never forget.

Whatever your style is important that you fight fair, taking into consideration your spouse. If you don't learn this, you will leave behind a trail of hurt, anger, disrespect, fear, disappointment, and unresolved conflicts behind you. If you learn how to fight fair, you will understand your spouse better, and in the end, you will find yourself growing closer rather than more distant. It is important to note the following:

1. Choose the right time and place: most fights occur when a spouse is tired, hungry, or stressed. These are not good times to fight because is easy to be irrational in these situations. It's also important not to fight in public or front of the kids. Conflicts in public bring unneeded embarrassment or humiliation, while in front of the kids can undermine your sense of parental unity and their sense of security. Should it happen in front of the kids, be sure to apologize in front of them.
2. Show respect: Watch your volume. Shouting can be humiliating and intimidating. Besides when the volume level rises, a fight can easily escalate and get out of control. You also need to choose your words carefully and respectfully. Name-calling will rarely result in anything positive. The goal of a conflict is to attack the problem and not the person. Once this is reversed be sure to cause another problem sooner or later.
3. Deal with an issue at a time: too often couples skip from one issue to the next without solving anything. In the midst of a disagreement, it's easy to get off track. One topic leads to another and soon you have no idea where you started, especially if you have so many unresolved issues shoved under the carpet. Always stay on one issue, resolve and move on.
4. Stay in the present: don't focus on things that happened in the past, whether a month or even a day ago. It is hard enough fighting about "now" issues. Most people think they have great memories but that's not the truth. The more time elapses from an event, the more potential there is for

distortion, reinterpretation, and just plain forgetfulness. So, try your best to stick to the present and not the past.

5. Never interrupt the other: it can be frustrating and annoying when trying to explain a point and your spouse won't let you finish or has already jumped to a conclusion. To solve a problem, try not to interrupt and listen to understand and not to respond.
6. End with resolution: a lot of couples have ongoing fights and are no closer to resolution than when they began. Remember that the purpose of marital conflict is to resolve something and not to win. Be willing to change, be willing to accept the other person's flaws, or be willing to accept and move on. resolutions are not always easy so make sure to talk about things very properly.
7. Always make up after a fight: often you have to apologize before you can make up. During a fight, things are said or done that aren't in the best interest of the marriage. Apologize for these and be ready to reconnect. After every fight, make it a point to do something special, go on a date, kiss, make love, hug, pray………do anything that reconnects or reaffirms the love.

Every couple has disagreements, but these don't have to be negative. We are all created uniquely and will approach life from different perspectives. You don't always have to agree to have a good marriage, positive fights can teach you a lot about each other and even yourselves. As you learn how to fight fair, build a relationship that can last as long as you both can live.

Prayer:

Dear God
When my love and I disagree, help me to fight fair. Forgive me for the times I get so wrapped up in winning that I forget about my spouse's feelings, priorities, or needs. Forgive me for my selfishness, my insensitivity, and my stubbornness.

Show me how to fight with respect. Empower me to show peace, love, patience, and gentleness in the midst of each conflict.

Teach me to resolve every fight graciously. Soften my heart and open my eyes to what will be best for both of us.

Help us to respond more maturely going forward.
Amen.

Passage
Romans 12:17
Never pay evil for evil to anyone. Do things in such a way that everyone can see you are honorable.

FORGIVE

It is in our DNA to hurt people unknowingly or knowingly or even as revenge. In every marriage, there are times you may hurt each other. You might say or do something that does not go down well with the other. You might be insensitive or rude. You may betray your spouse's trust or trample on their emotions. You may fail to defend, protect, honor, or love your partner. There are hundreds and thousands of ways to hurt each other. Sometimes you are keenly aware of your actions, other times your spouse suffers in silence whiles you naively move along, obviously to the hurt you've left behind.

Marriage is like a dance, no matter how careful you are, periodically you are going to step on your partner's feet. Some people have sensitive feet whiles others have tough feet, no matter which one, hurt still happens. If you step on the foot, it is important to seek forgiveness. If you have been stepped on, it's best for you and your marriage if you grant forgiveness. Without forgiveness, the hurt builds and the dance stops. Forgiveness allows you to reconnect in a positive way and dance along once more.

Forgiveness is not always easy especially if the partner involved isn't remorseful, but it is necessary. You seek forgiveness because you love your spouse and you don't want to cause pain. You grant forgiveness because you realize there have been times you have been forgiven and there will be times in the future you will need to be forgiven once more.

Since none of us is a perfect husband or wife, we are bound to find ourselves in plenty of situations that require forgiveness. This involves swallowing your pride and taking responsibility for what you did even if you did it unwittingly. One thing to note is stepping on a toe involves pain, whether accidentally or not.

If you are serious about showing love to your spouse, you will seek forgiveness for every offense. This begins by acknowledging what you have done. Don't justify the offense or come up with excuses. That will only make the situation worse. Even if you feel like your spouse was responsible for 90% of the problem, you must take responsibility for your part. Then accept that you have hurt the one that you fell in love with and married. Try to see the situation from both views/sides. Let his/her hurt and let it become your hurt. As you feel your spouse's hurt and pain, you will begin to regret the wound you have created.

Once you acknowledge the problem, you must go to your spouse and humbly apologize. Most men assume that with time the wife will let it go but trust me, the pain lingers on. Most women also assume sex will heal the wound but it doesn't. a simple sorry does the trick. Tell your spouse specifically why you were wrong so he/she will realize you take the situation seriously. Let them know you are very sorry for hurting them. Ask "will you forgive me?".

with these words, you take responsibility for your actions and submit to your spouse's mercy.

Even if you have done everything perfectly to this point, your spouse might not be ready to forgive. Some people can forgive easily and quickly, whiles others need more to work on their thoughts and feelings. Be patient.

The last step to seeking forgiveness is to change your behavior. Unfortunately, actions always speak louder than words. Your intentions might be great, but what your spouse wants is to be assured that she won't be hurt again. Trust is built when you and your spouse act in a trustworthy manner. To do this you must develop a plan, prepare for what might cause you to fail, keep yourself accountable to, at least, one person besides your spouse, and pray together for success.

As you seek forgiveness, you open the door to healing and togetherness. If you refuse to seek forgiveness, you slam the door to your spouse's feelings and block your relationship from growing.

Couples step on each other's feet many times every day. That's why we need to be quick to seek forgiveness. If you sense a wall being built between you and your spouse, find out if you have offended or hurt them. If you have, make it right.
The flip side of this coin is granting forgiveness. Refusing to forgive traps us in our pain and keeps us from healing and having peace of mind. Without forgiveness, trust can't be

regained and the relationship begins to die. Maybe you can ask yourself these questions:

- Does he deserve to be forgiven? Probably not.
- Will he do it again? Maybe
- Should you forgive him? Definitely
- Why? Because it is the right thing to do.
- When should you forgive him? A.S.A.P
- When should you trust him? Not until he proves himself trustworthy

And yet the hardest question is this: how do I forgive him? Start by admitting that you are hurt. Be honest. Don't deny the pain. That will ultimately make things worse. Don't exaggerate it either. Accurately facing your hurts prepares you to forgive.

Forgiveness is a decision. Facing your hurt helps you to know what you are forgiving. In this way, forgiveness frees you from being controlled by the pain. You forgive not to get your spouse off the hook but to help you to be healthy and to restore your relationship. Forgiveness means "to give something up." At the point of forgiveness, you let go of the poisons that are accompanying the hurt: anger, hatred, disgust, bitterness, fear, resentment, depression, confusion, and alienation.

Forgiveness is a decision to look forward instead of backward. By doing this, you are making four promises to yourself and your spouse:

1. I will not dwell on this incident
2. I will not bring up this incident again and use it against you.
3. I will not talk to others about the incident
4. I will not allow my bitterness about this incident to hurt our relationship.

Making these promises is not easy. Sometimes you need to ask God to help you forgive. Other times you need to think of all the hurtful things you've done to others and how they have forgiven you. If you are still stuck, consider how God has forgiven you a thousand times.

Now is the time to forgive your spouse and move on. Forgiveness allows you to a new beginning. There are days we all need a fresh start. So, repair your relationship, renew your love, and reestablish your dream of what could be.

Every house accumulates garbage, and so does marriage. Marriage tends to accumulate hurts and all types of pain. Forgiveness is simply taking out the garbage. Every day you injure each other. Every day you need to take out the garbage. But some of us have allowed the hurt to pile up for months. Some even for a year, then you act surprised when things don't smell good.

If you don't seek forgiveness and grant forgiveness, your marriage will start to rot. With time it will stink. Some couples seem to think that if their marriage starts smelling, they need to move to another "house." But the solution is so much simpler. *If you want a sweet-smelling relationship, take out the garbage.*

Prayer:

Dear God
Thank you for forgiving me for all the wrong things I have thought, said, and done. Even when I did not deserve forgiveness, you gave it freely with no strings attached. I want to be more like you.
Teach me to be more sensitive to the one I love. When I hurt my spouse, help me to be quick to seek forgiveness. Give me the courage and the humility to take responsibility with no excuse or justification. Help me to feel the pain I cause. Place the perfect words in my clumsy mouth, words that might not bring help and healing.
Make me realize that to hurt the one you gave me is to hurt you. Show me how to give grace, regardless of whether or not my mate deserves it. When my spouse hurts me, give me the ability to forgive quickly and completely, and sincerely, just as you have forgiven me
Build in me a forgiving heart.
Amen.

Passage
Colossians 3:3
You must make allowance for each other's faults and forgive the person who offends you. Remember, the Lord forgave you, so you must forgive others.

WELCOME EACH OTHER HOME

Traditionally women are to be stay-at-home mums to take care of the home and also be taken good care of by a hard-working man. My grandma once explained to me how she will dress up and perfume herself, and make grandpa's favorite meal each day to keep her marriage interesting by greeting her man at the front door with a welcome home kiss. She explained that he worked hard and the home needed to be a place he could relax. If someone doesn't feel positive about coming home, they are going to look for excuses to stay away. Most couples have not learned the secret power of a warm, positive welcome home because of this too many spouses find excuses to come home late.

In a world in which both spouses are working hard and contributing to the out keep of the home, it is not only the wife's responsibility to make the home welcoming, it is the responsibility of both spouses. There is always too much, there are friends who want to get together, there are hobbies that would be fun to do and there are meetings that must be attended. By themselves, there is nothing wrong with these activities, but if they are used to avoiding coming home, then there is a serious problem.

What happens the fifteen minutes of arriving home sets the tone and mood for the rest of the evening. If you return home to someone glad and excited to see you, you are happy to be there. When your greetings are responded to positively, with excitement, you are happy to always come home to that. If you are ignored and met with a list of everything that went wrong while you were gone, you begin to wish either you were somewhere else or delayed in coming home. When things are negative at home, you tend to look for a more positive place.

But let's also be realistic, things at home can't always be smooth. Always try to keep in touch with your partner. In doing this you will know who gets home first and what to expect.

Welcoming each other home is something that can transform your relationship and set the mood for better conversations though it might not always come naturally. If you are at home, anticipate when your beloved will arrive and create a welcome he/she will appreciate. If your spouse likes orders, try and give orders if he/she comes home hungry, and have some dinner ready, if your spouse loves peace and quietness, find a calm room for them to relax, if they love to be hugged and kissed and embraced, do exactly that. In short, tailor your welcome to what your spouse enjoys most.

On the other hand, always use your travel time to get a positive attitude. Slow down, clear all the negative thoughts, think about positive things, plan how to show love to your spouse, practice compliments and finally relax and pray for a good attitude. On your way home, try to relax, and consider all you have to be thankful for, when you get home, leave the work stress and frustration at the front door before you enter. Think of compliments you will like to say and fun things you will like to do. Psych yourself up so that you are excited to be home, when you step through the door, let your spouse know you are glad to finally be where you belong.

There are two major problems that couples with regard to coming home face. Both of these tendencies can destroy your sense of togetherness.

Firstly, there is the exhaustion factor. After a tedious day spent on the job, running errands, and or caring for the kids, a couple gets worn out. Too often a husband and a wife all their energy during the day and they give each other only what is left over. At the end of the day, all they have is exhaustion: tired meals, tired fun, tired talk, and even tired sex. The solution is to pace themselves and save some energy for a quality evening.

Secondly, there is the isolation factor. This is a tendency that strikes more men than women. They get home after a long day and want a break from people. So, they pull away from their partner to read newspapers, watch television, play on their phones or computers, or whatever solitary activity they enjoy most. The only way to overcome this is to commit to spending more time together talking and having fun. Women on the other hand want to come home after a stressful day with hugs and kisses. Don't let hobbies, special interests or relaxation take priority over the person you have chosen to spend your years and life with.

If partners who get home first are to welcome the other with loving enthusiasm, you would be surprised at the positive impact it would have on marriages. Couples will suddenly yearn to spend more time together and home will truly become a place of joy, comfort, and peace.

Prayer:

Dear God,
Forgive me for those days that I get so wrapped up in my agenda that I don't actively, lovingly welcome my spouse home. Help me to make my partner's homecoming the highlight of their day.
Plant in my heart the desire to come home with a great attitude to love my spouse unconditionally.
Teach me how to make my home a haven of joy, peace, and faith.
Show me how to create a safe harbor and refuge that I close to my heart – a place where the storms of life will not damage our love.
Direct me in ways that will make each homecoming special and all that follows it positive, encouraging, and delightful.
Make us a blessing to each other.
Amen.

Passage
1 Peter 5: 12
Great each other in Christian Love.

There is nothing nicer than being greeted with a hug and a kiss, discussing work stress, and finally showering together to relax each other.

GO TO BED AT THE SAME TIME/ TOGETHER

I am amazed at how many couples go to bed at different times. Maybe it's normal, but it is not necessarily healthy for a vital marriage. Too many couples live parallel lives. They spend most of their time doing different jobs, different hobbies and talking with different friends. If a couple isn't careful, this creates a distant marriage. Sure, partners might eat together, go to church together or even sleep on the same bed, but they have lost their sense of closeness. Some even sleep in separate rooms.

When you go to bed at the same time, you create a perfect opportunity to reconnect and rebuild the togetherness. To end the day together is a reminder that the two of you are one. So, set aside some quality time just before you go to bed. Make this time a special time. Go into your bedroom together and close the door, shutting out all the busyness, stress, and distractions of the world.

Research shows that the last thing on your mind as you to sleep is processed by your brain all night long. If you are unhappy or angry with your spouse as you lay in bed, there is a good chance you will continue those thoughts in the dream/ sleep world. Your brain never shuts, it is as active during the night as it is during the day. Thus, if you go to sleep with positive thoughts and feelings towards your spouse, those feelings and thoughts get repeated and deeply embedded. This will help you to feel great about your mate when awake.

Ephesians 4:26 – Do not let the sun go down while you are still angry. In short, don't argue in bed. Resolve all your issues, or at least let go of them before it gets too late at night. Many are those who save their arguments for their bedroom but I would encourage you to keep it out of the bedroom. Let your room be the most positive in your room, a pleasant place of peace to which you and your partner long to escape. A place of sweet good memories. Clear out the clutter, give it a fresh coat of paint, add some romantic touches and music, and create an atmosphere that you both enjoy.

After a stressful day at work, the half-hour when the kids are asleep, etc can be the best part of the day. If you are creative with this special time, it will build wonderful memories, intimate moments, and a better marriage. Can you imagine having a different activity each day?

Monday night: give each other a back rub and or shower together.

Tuesday night: talk about old times or read together.

Wednesday night: play truth or dare.

Thursday night: Cuddled up in bed, watch a short romantic movie together.

Friday night: Go on a date.

Saturday night: Talk about plans, targets, etc.

Sunday night: do a devotional together, committing the week to the Almighty's hands.

By going into the bedroom and getting into bed together, you can create a time for sharing. Lying side by side, looking into each other's eyes, making real efforts to share what is on your heart. At the end of the day, your defenses are down and this allows your heart to be more open. Don't miss this opportunity as there is much more than an opportunity to share; it is an opportunity to make your marriage better.

Prayer:

Dear God
Protect my evening time, when the sun goes down and the world grows quiet.
Allow this to be the time that draws my beloved and me closer together, a time we anticipate, protect, and treasure.
Teach me how to make our time at night positive, listening, loving, and sharing.
Remind me to reach out to my spouse at the end of the day no matter how stressful it was. Motivate me to make our bedroom a place that draws us in so we can truly connect, appreciate each other, and grow deeper in love.

Forgive me for all the times I have gone to bed alone or allowed my partner to do so alone.
Thank you for giving me a special someone with whom I can share my bedtime.

Passage
Ecclesiastes 4: 11
And on a cold night, two under the same blanket can give warmth to each other. But how can one be warm alone?

DEVELOP MUTUAL FRIENDS

Every couple needs mutual friends. My attention was drawn to this in a conversation with one female colleague and I realized is one of the key things we ignore in a relationship. Years ago, before our culture became so mobile, most married couples lived close to their parents, grandparents, uncles, aunts, and cousins. Many stayed in the same community all their lives and few moved away from strong families and lifelong friends. That was the time people grew up knowing the names of their neighbors and building close relationships with those around them. Because of this, there was a built-in support system. These days we have become so independent and busy that we are disconnected from family and community. Therefore, mutual friends are more important than ever before in helping a marriage succeed.

Friends can help you through the rough times in a marriage and they can enrich the positive times in your relationship. Friends can make a good marriage better, by supporting and protecting all that is important.

On the flip side, friends who are not emotionally healthy and stable can create a lot of tension and frustration in a relationship and sometimes can even tear it apart.

Five aspects of friendship can create stress and potential destruction in your marriage:

Lack of friends: If you don't have any friends, you have no support system for your relationship. That means that you will be looking to your spouse to meet all your social, interactive, and emotional needs. No partner can meet every need. For example, many women have higher communication needs whiles men have higher competitive needs. Therefore, women will want to meet frequently to communicate and men, often to compete. Having friends often takes some of the pressure of differing needs of the marriage.

Separate friends: Often a husband will have his male friends and a wife will have her female friends. This is healthy and normal in most situations. However, if you start spending more time with your friends than you do with your spouse or if you find yourself enjoying certain friends more than you do your spouse, you are headed for trouble. Separate friends can be good unless they create a wedge in your togetherness with your spouse. If your friends become your spouse's friends, there is less potential for division.

Negative friends: We are all influenced by our friends. When that influence is positive, everybody is happy. but if your friends speak poorly of marriage or have negative qualities that might weaken or threaten your marriage, you need to avoid them regardless of how wonderful they are. You also need to beware of friends who don't like, respect, or approve of your spouse. Even if these friends are right, such attitudes need to be handled in a considerate, constructive way. If your friends are rude to your spouse, minimize contact with them. Lastly, friends who have a more relative value system than you have can easily lead you in a direction you will someday regret.

Opposite-sex friends: Maybe you relate better to members of the opposite sex and maybe your closest friends are of the opposite sex, but these relationships pose a potential danger to your marriage. They can trigger jealousies and run the risk of becoming more intimate than either of you may have intended. Be careful about spending too much time alone with those of the opposite sex., especially sharing deep emotions and difficulties or doing fun and recreational activities together. Even though a situation may be perfectly innocent, it can have a questionable appearance. Besides, innocent situations can easily escalate into not-so-innocent situations. Don't be naïve.

Too many friends: Some people are so social and extroverted that they fill their lives with as many friends as possible. While these friends may be positive and healthy, too many of them can create problems. Too many friends will start to consume more and more of your time, along with more and more of your energy. And soon you will have less time and energy for your marriage. Remember, o your spouse is your primary companion, don't let anything determine this relationship. Too much of a good thing is not healthy. That's true of chocolate, sports, and even friends.

Healthy friendships take a lot of pressure off marriage and strengthen it in valuable ways. Friends provide a place to vent frustration, check out perceptions, talk about things our partners have no interest in, and participate in activities our spouse doesn't care about.

Finding another couple with whom to spend time has many benefits you may never have thought of. Yet in choosing another couple it is important that you both feel comfortable with the choice. Often two wives will connect and enjoy their time together so much that they assume their husbands will naturally become good friends. Sometimes such friendship develops, but sometimes it doesn't. be sensitive to the fact that some personalities don't click, regardless of how hard you push and pray. Once you find another couple with whom you both click, you will realize what a treasure you have found.

Here are some of the many benefits of having healthy, mutual couple friends:

- They remind you of what's normal in a relationship
- They encourage habits, activities, and attitudes that build a good marriage
- They provide a place to vent and work through everyday marital frustrations
- They confront wrong, foolish, illegal, and insensitive behavior
- They offer opportunities for fun social interactions
- They bring new ideas for strengthening, improving, and revitalizing your marriage.

Mutual friends can also encourage you to make it through the rough times by being supportive of both.

Prayer:

Dear God,
Thank you for the good friends in our lives and thank you Lord for being the best of all friends
Bring into my marriage healthy, positive, mutual friends. Help us to appreciate those friends and give back to them the good gift they have given us.

Provide us with the courage and wisdom to say no to friends who might damage or undermine our marriage. Create in us a bold and faithful heart that will not hesitate to protect our marriage from risky relationships, even if those friends are nice, attractive, fun, and exciting to be with.

Show us how to be good friends with our spouse, building in us the qualities that will encourage and enrich the marriages of couples we come across.

Make us good examples of what you want marriages to be.
Amen

Passage
Proverbs 17:17
A friend is always loyal.

Passage
Sit with your spouse and talk about friends you both have. Look at the 5 aspects of friendship that can create stress and find out if any of their friends fit into the category. Together explore options of how you can overcome this challenge.

DATE TIME

I remember the early days of our marriage when my husband and I will spend weekends away from home and the kids. The hotel room was always filled with love and love songs. We will take strolls, and dance together……it was always fantastic.

Every time I think about these dates, I am reminded of our love. Dating is a way to express your appreciation, create romance, show respect, add significance, and share the love. Spending time together as a couple is vital to the relationship.

Couples don't usually decide to stop dating, it just happens. Sometimes the responsibilities of work or family take all your time. Sometimes the hectic pace of life takes all your energy, leaving you too tired and exhausted for much else. Other times you just get lazy and fall into a rut of inactivity and distraction. Then there are the other big logistical problems - no money. But if you want a great marriage, you won't use any of these excuses, for love always finds a way. How can something that once was so easy become so hard? It doesn't have to be! All you have to do is remember a few simple principles:

Schedule it: if you don't schedule dates, you won't have dates. I know a couple that makes every Friday after work a date time. It however doesn't have to be in the evening to be a date. If it is more convenient, schedule breakfast or midday dates.

It is however amazing how expensive dating can get if you aren't careful, especially in this hard economy. So, make sure you write weekly dates into your budget. So aside money that can only be used for going out together. Don't think of this as wasted or frivolous money, it's an investment in the most important thing in your life, your marriage. And if you don't make a regular investment, you might find your relationship going bankrupt. But if finances are tight, this doesn't mean you can't date. There are thousands of things you can do for little or no money. You can go for a drive, walk through a garden, play tennis, etc. the essence is to spend quality time together, creating memories.

Trade it: what should you do and who should plan it? This s where some couples get stuck. Others get frustrated because one partner ends up doing all the work of arranging the dates. This sometimes leaves the impression that the other partner doesn't care about dating or isn't willing to put forth much effort. To solve this problem, I encourage couples to trade-off. The husband plans and make all the arrangement for one date. This includes deciding on the activity, arranging for child care, and planning the meals. Then you repeat the process. When your partner is in charge of the date, cooperate and be positive even if what he/she chooses isn't your favorite thing to do. The next week you will be in charge.

Energize it: if you keep going to the same restaurant, it soon loses its special appeal. Try new things. The best dates are those that hold at least some uniqueness, wonder, variety, or creativity.

Develop new ideas and even if you don't enjoy them, a new memory would have been created from them. Doing things that are new or different energizes your dating and keeps your love life alive. Boredom can kill your spirit and your relationship. Keep the fire burning.

Communicate it: the most important thing about your dates is not what you do or where you go but how you communicate. Talking and listening, just the two of you, without distraction, can be one of the most positive times of your week. So whatever you do, make sure intimate, honest, and deep-down communication is part of it. When you know each other intimately, your marriage becomes more emotionally rewarding. Share your heart and discover the heart of your mate. Get close, but avoid talking about schedules, money, children, and complaints. Save that for later. Keep your date talk focused on learning more about one another's hearts and desires.

Romance it: Romance is not optional. If you ignore it, your dates will suffer and ultimately your marriage will suffer. Too many couples let romance slip away because is not easy. But easy or not, it is important. Also, note that romance is not all about sex

Enjoy it: When you go on such dates, do everything possible to please your partner and make it a great experience. Know what they like and where they like to go. Make your time together the best, fill it with joy, closeness, and laughter. Show your spouse what love is all about.

It is dating that brought you together with your partner and it can keep you together. Dating pulls you above the ordinary, allowing you special time to communicate and connect. Enjoying some type of date every week will improve your marriage and help you to appreciate each other even more.

> *Prayer:*
>
> *Dear God,*
> *Encourage me to date, my spouse, more often — really date like before we were married. Place this desire deep in my heart and help me turn it into reality.*
> *Forgive me for the times I have treated my beloved as kindly and especially as she deserves. Forgive me for the excuses I have given for not going out on regular dates.*
> *Show me how to date generously and selflessly, always demonstrating by attitude, action, and words how special my mate truly is to me*
> *Teach me how to date with so much chivalry that it overflows into every aspect of my marriage. Give me a renewed feeling of romance in my heart and let it shine on my spouse even when I am not in my best mood.*
> *Help me to remember you in all that we do. Bring us closer to each other, and you with every date.*
> *Thank you for being the source of love.*
> *Amen.*

Passage

Songs of Songs 2:2-4

Young man: "yes, compared to other women, my beloved is like a lily among thorns"

Young woman: "And compared to other youths, my lover is like the finest apple tree in the orchard. I am seated in his delightful shade, and his fruit is delicious to eat. He brings me to the banquet hall, so everyone can see how much he loves me.

Practice

1. Ask your spouse out on a date to do something you know they will enjoy, even if it isn't your first preference.
2. Sit down together and schedule two dates for the upcoming month. Talk about how you can make this happen in terms of money, planning, interest, and any other details that might sabotage your plans.

MAKE LOVE

How can something so incredible for some couples be so difficult for others?

Sexuality is one of the most private and sensitive aspects of a marriage. For some couples, it is wonderful, for others it is overstated and for still others, it's a curse.

Men and women are wired differently; this is especially true in the sexual arena. For many men, physical intimacy opens the heart to emotional intimacy. For some women, the opposite is usually true- emotional intimacy opens the heart to physical intimacy. Therefore, if there has just been a conflict, a man might want a sexual connection. That is his way of resolving everything. For a woman, sex might be the last thing on her mind. She needs to feel peace with her husband before she has any desire to make love to him.

Another common difference involves arousal. Men can easily be aroused and feel amorous very quickly, regardless of the time and setting. Women often build towards amorous feelings and are aroused slowly, with time and setting significantly related to the process. Men tend to operate like a light switch; they are either turned on or turned off. Women tend to operate more like dimmer switches: they slowly turn the lights up.

The third difference involves stress. For a woman to feel

arousal, she usually needs to relax. In fact, for many women the greater the relaxation, the greater the arousal. They need to be able to clear their minds, relax their bodies, and focus positively on the one they love. Any potential distraction (such as children, strange noises, physical discomfort, self-consciousness, or anxiety) can kill the mood and steal their arousal. For a man, stress often increases his arousal. The greater the stress, the more desire he feels and the more intense his drive for sexual release. A man may become so focused at this point that he doesn't even notice those things that distract his wife. Only after climax does he relax, and then he often falls asleep. Women, on the other hand, frequently find they feel energized after lovemaking.

Because of all couples' inevitable differences, sexual communication is very important. Yet most couples rarely talk about their physical relationship their needs, expectations, preferences, fears, comfort zones, and sensitivities. With a little communication, a couple can avoid a lot of confusion, hurt, and misunderstanding. Talking brings you closer, and though it might not solve all your sexual struggles, it at least allows you to understand them better. As you talk, remember that healthy lovemaking is not selfish or greedy. It is patient. It is caring. It is neither pushy nor demanding. It always puts the needs and sensitivities of your partner above your own.
Sexuality involves "the three G's." First, sex is good. "God saw all that he had made, and it was very good" (Genesis 1:31, NIV). God created sex, and when it is expressed unselfishly within the boundaries of marriage, it is a mutual blessing.

Sex is glue. "For this reason, a man will leave his father and mother and be united to his wife, and they will become one flesh" (Genesis 2:24, NIV). Sexuality protects a couple from outside temptations and bonds them closer together than any other relationship can.

Sex is a gift. "The wife's body does not belong to her alone but also to her husband. In the same way, the husband's body does not belong to him alone but also to his wife" (1 Corinthians 7:4, NIV), Freely giving yourself to you spouse with no expectations in return is true romance.

Keeping "the three G's' in mind, all couples should make it a priority to make love at least once a week. Try not to make love simply out of despite, habit, or duty. Make love in a way that shows love. To do this, every couple must look at the big picture. Lovemaking is a lot more than a few minutes of physical intimacy; it should be a well-thought-out event.

Lovemaking consists of at least six very important components. If you want a positive sexual connection with your spouse, pay attention to each of these components:

1. **Context:** A couple's interaction in the twelve hours before lovemaking sets the context for closeness. Be kind and caring. Pay attention to each other. Remember that sincere, meaningful lovemaking grows from a context of love.

2. **Atmosphere:** Draw each other into romance by creating an atmosphere that feeds all five senses. Here are a few suggestions:
Hearing: romantic music
Sight: candlelight, flowers
Touch: bubble bath, satin sheets, massage oil
Taste: chocolate, fruit, sparkling cider
Smell: scented candles, special perfume/ cologne
3. **Connection:** Someone once said that women spell sex "T-A-L-K"
This has more truth than many men realize. Talking can warm your wife and help her to be more open to you. When a guy shares his heart, listens, shows thoughtfulness, touches and caresses his wife in nonsexual ways, and helps her to relax, then she feels connected.
4. **Foreplay:** This is where a couple crosses the line from emotional intimacy to physical intimacy. Set aside at least ten to fifteen minutes for foreplay. Some women say that this component of lovemaking is the most satisfying. Learn how to give a massage that truly relaxes and brings you in sync with each other. Does your spouse enjoy back, leg, or foot rubs? Do what brings the most pleasure. Then move to cuddling and kissing. Husbands, take your time and don't rush it. Wives, if he moves too fast, don't get frustrated. He's just more aroused than you are. Calmly and gently redirect him.
5. **Interplay:** Here is where arousal reaches its climax. Allow yourself to become one with each other. Sexual togetherness is sacred and brings a couple vulnerably close to one another.

It is a symbol of unity and commitment. Treasure it and keep it pure. Focus on bringing pleasure and fulfillment to your partner. Remember that love is patient and places your beloved before yourself.

6. **Follow-through:** Never allow lovemaking to end abruptly or negatively. A bad ending can ruin a great book or an excellent movie. This is equally true with your most intimate times. After your sexual time, lie in each other's arms. Talk for a moment or two, complimenting and thanking your spouse for sharing her body. Then create closure on this most precious time with a gentle kiss or a prayer or even both.

Sexuality should bring a couple closer, but all too often it does the opposite. If it has been a while since you've made love, something is probably wrong that you need to work out. I realize there are times of exhaustion, health difficulties, or separation that might create a period of abstinence. But this should be the exception, not the rule. If there is any difficulty in this area, don't ignore it. Talk to a physician, psychologist, counselor, or pastor. Remember, making love is an important way to show your love. And as you show your love, your marriage will grow stronger, deeper, and more exciting.

Prayer:

Dear God,
Help me to understand the needs, expectations, preferences, fears, comfort zones, and sensitivities of the one I love. Then teach the two of us to talk about this aspect of our life in a way that brings us closer

together.

When frustrations arise in our lovemaking, show us how to be patient and understanding toward each other.

Thank you for creating sex as a symbol of our marriage. Thank you for making sex good. Help us to keep it that way. Help it to keep us close for the rest of our lives. Thank you for making sex a gift. Help us to give it with meaning generosity, and selflessness. Forgive me for the times I have placed sexual pleasure above love, stimulation above sensitivity, and my needs above my spouse's. Show me how I might be the best sexual partner possible for my spouse.
Amen

Passage
1 CORINTHIANS 7:3
The husband should not deprive his wife of sexual intimacy, which is her right as a married woman, nor should the wife deprive her husband.

Practice
Sit down together and talk honestly about "the three G's." Discuss how gender differences and personality differences may affect your love life.
Then agree on a level of sexual frequency and an approach

with which you both feel comfortable.

Do all you can to assure a positive context and an emotional connection before you initiate sexual times. Try giving a heartfelt compliment, making a romantic phone call, surprising her with her favorite "something", drink, or dessert, showing an extra portion of kindness, or simply doing whatever you can to make the day positive for your spouse.
The next time you consider a sexual connection, set up a romantic
atmosphere that includes at least four of the five senses. Commit to at least ten to fifteen minutes of foreplay before making
love. During this time, cuddle, kiss, relax and communicate to your spouse how much you love him/her.

PRAY FOR YOUR SPOUSE

A pastor once said that prayer is the first step to meeting any challenge. I believe that we all have a responsibility to pray for our spouses daily. Don't just pray when you are feeling loving, happy, or appreciative. Pray when you are: lonely, empty, broken frustrated, fighting, angry, disgusted, disappointed, or disconnected.

A friend of mine once said that prayer should be the key that opens each morning and the bolt that locks up each night. If every spouse prayed sincerely for his partner each morning and evening, marriages would be much healthier. But often it's not the person who's being prayed for who changes the most, it's the person who prays.

There are at least ten things that anyone married should pray about:

Yourself: Pray that you will be the best spouse you can be. Ask forgiveness for those times you have been selfish or insensitive. Focus on loving your partner more, always treating him with courtesy and compassion. Pray that you will change your negative or neglectful attitude. As we improve our words and behavior, we pave the way for our spouses to make similar changes.

A pastor once said that prayer is the first step to meeting any challenge. I believe that we all have a responsibility to pray for our spouses daily. Don't just pray when you are feeling loving, happy, or appreciative. Pray when you are: lonely, empty, broken frustrated, fighting, angry, disgusted, disappointed, or disconnected.

A friend of mine once said that prayer should be the key that opens each morning and the bolt that locks up each night. If every spouse prayed sincerely for his partner each morning and evening, marriages would be much healthier. But often it's not the person who's being prayed for who changes the most, it's the person who prays.

There are at least ten things that anyone married should pray about:

Yourself: Pray that you will be the best spouse you can be. Ask forgiveness for those times you have been selfish or insensitive. Focus on loving your partner more, always treating him with courtesy and compassion. Pray that you will change your negative or neglectful attitude. As we improve our words and behavior, we pave the way for our spouses to make similar changes.

Your marriage: Pray that the two of you will find a oneness that will bring you closer together. Too often couples drift apart from each other and lose that special sense of love and joy that was present at the beginning. Pray that you both will make your marriage a priority, committing time to understand each other and placing your spouse's needs above your own.

Safety: No one knows for sure what danger lies around the next corner. Pray for your spouse's safety and protection in a world that is more dangerous than any of us wish to admit.

Health: Many of us try to eat healthily, exercise regularly, take vitamins daily, and visit a doctor when needed. These are good things, but prayer has more potential power than all four of these combined. Pray for your partner's health and strength. Pray that her body would be able to fight minor illnesses and major diseases and that her life would be long and free from sickness.

Stress: Life is full of pressure and expectations. We race from one point to another, trying to force more into a day than is reasonable. This stress frequently steals our peace and enjoyment. It makes us irritable and impatient. It opens doors to worry, depression, burnout, and all sorts of physical symptoms. Pray that your spouse will not be overwhelmed by the stress of life.

Pray that he will be able to relax and find contentment in all he does.

Temptations: We all have times when we're tempted to do things that are not good for us or our marriage. Some people face such strong temptations that they have what is called an addictive personality. Others have less potent but equally dangerous temptations. Given the right situation, any of us could fall into temptation. Know your partner's weaknesses and struggles whether it's alcohol, food, pornography, overspending, drugs, gambling, or anything else. Then pray for your partner. Work: Some partners struggle which laziness and others struggle with workaholism. Neither extreme is healthy. Pray that your partner will find a balance in his work. Pray that it will bring him a sense of fulfillment. Our jobs, whether they're inside or outside the home, impact how we feel about ourselves and our marriages. Pray that your partner's job will be a positive part of his life, filling him with a sense of meaning purpose, and personal satisfaction.

Fears: We all have fears. These fears can be overwhelming and maybe even irrational. Know your partner's fears. Do they have to do with safety, finances, failure, or death? Pray that these fears will not paralyze your spouse but that she can work through them and overcome them. Also, pray that you can be patient and understanding, doing all that you can to help and bring comfort. Never ridicule or belittle your spouse for her fears. Be a source of reassurance and support.

Dreams: Every couple and all individuals need to have dreams. Without dreams, people grow discouraged, and life becomes empty or meaningless. Dreams add focus, excitement, joy, and hope. But dreams can easily be killed or deflated. Share your dreams and pray that your partner's dreams will come true. Encourage him and cheer him on. If he doesn't have a dream, help him to develop one. If he's given up on a dream, see if it can be resurrected. If you know his dreams, pray like crazy that they'll be fulfilled.

Faith: As you pray for your partner's faith, you are, praying for all of the previous nine areas. Faith impacts every aspect of one's life. If your partner struggles with her faith, don't preach or pressure her. Instead, pray and live an example of a godly life. I have heard hundreds of stories of how a spouse's persistent prayers opened the heart of a partner.

"More things are wrought by prayer than this world dreams of." Prayer can change the one who prays, one's marriage, and one's partner. Don't let a day pass without serious prayer. What can happen will surprise you, don't be limited to praying only for the ten suggested areas. Here are ten more to get you started:

- His past
- Her parenting
- His sexuality
- Her self-image
- His attitude
- Her words
- His example
- Her friendships
- His contentment
- Her priorities

Ultimately, prayer is your best protection. Going through marriage without prayer is like walking a high wire without a safety net. Don't be foolish.

Always remember that prayer succeeds when all else fails.

Prayer:

Prayer
Dear God,
Help me to be the best spouse I can be. Forgive me for all the times I have not prayed for my beloved.

When I am angry or frustrated with my spouse, remind me to pray rather than react. Remind me to pray for my partner every morning, every night, and anytime in between. Bring to my attention all the needs of my beloved. Teach me to pray deeply and sincerely and passionately for him. If there are other things my partner needs or wishes me to pray for, bring them to my mind.

Thank you for listening to my prayers and taking them seriously. Thank you for being a God who not only hears but also cares enough to answer.
Amen

Passage
EPHESIANS 6:18
Pray at all times and on every occasion in the power of the Holy Spirit.

Practice
- Ask your spouse how you could pray more effectively for his needs. Ask him if he would give you a weekly update of things for which you could pray.
- Find a quiet time and place where you can pray for yourself, pray for your attitude, your struggles, your bad habits, and anything you do that might hurt your spouse or your marriage.
- Set aside at least ten minutes each day to pray specifically for your spouse and nothing else. Among other things, be sure to pray for her safety, health, stress, temptations, work, fears, dreams, and faith.

TREASURE YOUR SPOUSE

Often it takes a crisis to realize what is of true value. Your spouse is a unique and special person with strengths and talents and potential. Too often, we take that person for granted. Too often we don't treasure a person until after he/she's gone. Then we finally realize how much he/she meant to us and how empty life will be without her. Now is the time to treasure your spouse.

Treasure him as your friend. Those couples that are healthiest have learned how to be good friends. We all need friends, and when your spouse is a friend, your marriage doubles in satisfaction. Friendship with your mate chases away your loneliness and turns your home into a haven. Friendship also provides an emotional and intellectual connection that deepens your marriage. Emotionally you are embraced and accepted. Intellectually you are respected, though you and your spouse may not always agree. These two connections within a marriage make a secure bond that will protect the marriage from many outside temptations.

If friendship is so powerful a force within marriage, what exactly is a friend? Friends enjoy spending time together. They accept each other, even when they disagree. Friends know what makes each other smile. They share their hopes, hurts, and deepest secrets without fear of rejection. Friends listen-really listen-with an ear bent on knowing the other person better.

They help each other out and are there when things get rough. Friends don't have to have it their way. They resolve conflicts and forgive each other. They are honest and trustworthy, kind and courteous, strong and gentle. Friends stand up for each other.

Treasure her as your encourager. Love believes the best about the other person. What you look for is usually what you find. If you search for beauty and integrity in your spouse, you will find it. If you encourage beauty and integrity, it will grow. The power of encouragement is often underestimated. Encouragement plants acorns and then helps them mature into oaks.

A friend of mine once told me, "I'm a much better person now than I was the day my husband and I got married."

"How did that come to be!" I asked.

"It was my husband," she said with tears in her eyes. "He believed in me when I had lost faith in myself. He loved me when I thought I was unlovable. He encouraged me every day of our marriage. Without him, I'd be lost. "Work hard to be your spouse's biggest encourager. Pay attention to her strengths and talents and interests. Be an optimist, and help your spouse believe how special and treasured she truly is. Dry her tears, nurture her potential, applaud her victories, and assist her in turning her dreams into reality.

Both husband and wife should be the top cheerleaders of each other. Your job is to encourage and build one other up.

Treasure him as your lover. To love and be loved is one of the greatest experiences a person can have. You and your spouse are lovers. This connection should reach out to include every aspect of love, from courtesy to romance to intimacy. Treasure your mate as your beloved, and daily show him the power of unconditional love. Every married person should memorize the definition of unconditional love, found in the love chapter of the Bible:

Love is patient and kind. Love is not jealous or boastful or proud or rude. Love does not demand its own way. Love is not irritable, and it keeps no record of when it has been wronged. It is never glad about injustice but rejoices whenever the truth wins out. Love never gives up, never loses faith, is always hopeful, and endures through every circumstance. Love will last forever.
1 CORINTHIANS 13:4-8

Every spouse should be a helper to his spouse. Marriage is a total, timeless commitment. It involves giving yourself fully to your spouse. Marriage involves sacrifice on your part, but in that sacrifice, you find purpose, meaning, and significance. You discover that treasuring your spouse over everything deepens your bond and your marriage.

Marriage is a miracle. As you treasure your spouse, he will treasure you. I've found that when I treasure someone, I get back two to three times more than what I have given. Treasure your partner in any way you can. Treasure your partner friend, as an encourager, and as a lover.

Prayer:

Dear God,
Forgive me for not treasuring my spouse as the most special and valuable gift you have given me.

Remind me that we are friends, and teach me how I might be a true friend in good times and bad.

Remind me that we are encouragers, and open my eyes daily to the many opportunities I have to build up and believe the best about my spouse.

Remind me that we are lovers, and guide me into an unconditional love that bears all things, believes all things, hopes all things, and endures all things.

Push me beyond my selfishness toward a commitment that is total and timeless.

Mold me into a spouse who knows how to truly treasure my mate. Give me the strength to treasure my partner beyond what is easy, normal, or humanly possible.
Amen

Passage

SONG OF SONGS 8.6-7

Place me like a seal over your heart. ... Love flashes like fire, the brightest kind of flame. Many waters cannot quench love, neither can rivers drown it. If a man tried to buy love with everything he owned, his offer would be utterly despised

Practice

1. Write a letter, in your style, describing how and why you treasure your spouse. Read to him what you have written, or print it out and give it to him.
2. Evaluate what kind of friend, encourager, and lover you have been to your partner in the past month. Determine what you need to do to improve in each of these areas.
3. Go to your spouse earnestly, humbly, and privately. Kneel before her, take her hand, and commit yourself. Commit yourself to treasure her, in any way possible, until the end of your days

WRAPPING UP

It baffles me to know that we go to school to learn a career, and how to carry ourselves but never really take our time to study marriage, an institution that we are to spend our entire life, even after retirement. Why then do we take it for granted?

www.ingramcontent.com/pod-product-compliance
Lightning Source LLC
Chambersburg PA
CBHW031835230426
43669CB00009B/1365